TRAINING SETTERS AND POINTERS
FOR FIELD TRIALS

Training Setters and Pointers for Field Trials

JOHN M. BEAZLEY
M.D., F.R.C.O.G.

ALFRED K. MANNERS
Trainer-handler

ARNOLD C. WHITE-ROBINSON
Trainer-handler

ARCO PUBLISHING COMPANY, INC.
New York

Published 1974 by Arco Publishing Company, Inc.,
219 Park Avenue South, New York, N.Y. 10003

Copyright © 1973 by John M. Beazley,
Alfred K. Manners, and Arnold C. White-Robinson

Library of Congress Catalog Card Number 72-94051

ISBN 0-668-02911-0

Printed in Great Britain

Colonel Arthur Sydney Balding, M.C., who has written the foreword to this book, has been an ardent and constant follower of setter and pointer field trials since 1925. From 1928 to 1968 he was an active participant in field trials in which he has won awards with pointers, English setters, and Irish setters and he has much knowledge of the working lines of these breeds. His administrative abilities have been invaluable in the promotion of several pointer and setter clubs. At present he is President of the International Gundog League Pointer and Setter Society; Vice-President of the English Setter Club; a member of the Kennel Club, on whose field trials sub-committee he formerly served; and a member of the Irish Setter Association, England; The Pointer Club; and the Setter and Pointer Club.

My colleagues and I will continue to be grateful to him for his guidance and support.

J.M.B.

CONTENTS

ILLUSTRATIONS

Tables

FOREWORD

The owners who met at Southill in Bedfordshire in 1865 with their pointers and setters and created field trials for gun dogs, could have had no conception of the extent to which the sport would spread in this and many other countries. Throughout succeeding years the four breeds have been bred selectively by generations of owners, and today puppies from proved lines of work are still available for newcomers to the sport.

The three authors of this book are all successful trainers and handlers of pointers and setters in field trials in the United Kingdom. Their object has been to write a manual of training to assist intending trainers with the preliminary schooling of their puppies. It is written especially for people who lack the assistance, locally, of an expert adviser, or ample training ground stocked with game. The comprehensive information will also be read with interest by others more experienced with pointers and setters.

Readers who contemplate participating in this sport are recommended to attend some field trial meetings first, where they can watch the dogs at work and talk to their handlers before reaching a decision. Those who then decide to take up the sport will find their recreation a challenge, involving much hard and concentrated work with little or no financial reward. The sport will, however, take them to some of the most beautiful parts of the country, off the beaten tourist tracks, and involve them in plenty of open air exercise among companions who share their interest.

On the day the first field trial award is won all the effort will have been worthwhile!

Those who share the love of working pointers and setters with the authors will appreciate the care with which they have compiled this book.

A. SYDNEY BALDING

PREFACE

The aim of this handbook is to provide would-be trainers of setters or pointers with a reliable source of information from which they may obtain guidance in the preparation of bird dogs for field trials. The book is written mainly for inexperienced enthusiasts who have neither estates stocked with game nor large kennels of well-schooled dogs. It is hoped, however, that other readers may also find herein something of interest and value.

The book is based on field trial incidents and comments of the field trial fraternity which I recorded during competitions after 1966. My co-authors have added their own wisdom and experience to these views so that, together, we hope the reader is presented with an up-to-date account of current views upon this fascinating field sport.

To those friends with whom it has been our privilege to share the pleasures and excitements, the frustrations and disappointments of many field trials, we express our gratitude and hope they will realize how important is the contribution which they have made to what is written here. To the Great Patrons of the sport, whose grounds have been offered so generously for field trials, we all express our sincerest thanks.

J.M.B.

1 · BIRD DOGS: THEIR PURPOSE AND STYLE

The true purpose of bird dogs is not solely to locate game birds but to find and raise them in such a way that they may be shot, leaving none behind. Unlike some questing dogs, e.g. spaniels or German short-haired pointers, which also retrieve the killed or wounded game, English setters, English pointers, Irish (Red) and Gordon (Black-and-tan) setters are used only to locate and subsequently to raise the hidden birds.

Although the purpose of all true questing dogs is the same, the manner in which each of them indicates the nearby presence of game differs slightly. With untold swiftness pointers freeze to immobility, adopting a stiff and classical stance, their flared nostrils held high to the wind, one forepaw bent, their tail rigid and held straight in line with their back (Plate 1). By contrast, setters, especially Irish setters, often take up a low crouching position before birds, or even lie close to the ground, indicating by the direction of their fixed gaze the position of the game (Plate 2). Their pose of intense interest, half crouching, is sometimes termed 'setting'. A rather different stance, altogether more upright, with the head and feathered tail still, but carried proudly erect, is commonly adopted by English setters (Plate 3).

Hunting over dogs

In his famous book, William Arkwright[1] differentiates sharply between the pleasure to be derived from hunting game with bird dogs and the entertainment of shooting game driven towards

[1] Arkwright, W., *The Pointer and His Predecessors* (London: A. L. Humphreys, 1902), p. 46.

B

the gun, a diversion now enjoyed by only a privileged few. Quoting from *Le Chasseur au chien d'arrêt* (1846), he says:

'The pleasure of the true sportsman commences when his dog meets him; Kings have no dogs, or rather no pointing dogs, and if they have, they don't use them:—two hundred beaters take their place. The pleasure increases when the animal makes a good point; Kings have never seen a dog on point,— an increasing stream of game flows before them. The sportsman delights in gathering his bird, in handling it, etc; Kings do not see the dead game nearer than twenty paces,—touch it never. Their business is to fire a thousand shots; a steam engine could do it as well. . . . You must search for game! If it comes to you, the pleasure is diminished. A pretty woman who offers herself, loses three quarters of her attractions. What do I say! She loses them all.'

In the same book Arkwright himself describes, in some detail, the true joy of handling bird dogs. He says (p. 136):

'Still of course, the chief glory of the sport is to shoot over a brace of raking pointers, matched for speed and style, sweeping over the rough places like swallows, and passing each other as if they were fine ladies not introduced. Let one of them get a point and the other will, as if connected by invisible wire, instantly point at him (i.e. back him); and as the pointing dog advances to make sure of the birds, the backer will do the same—often with an absolute mimicry of his leader's movements. When his Master has come to the spot, how proudly will the first dog march him up to the game with outstretched neck, flame in his eye, and foam at his lips, while his companion watches from a distance with perfect self-control; and, when the birds rise, both dogs instantly drop to the ground, not to move till the game is gathered, and they are bidden to resume their search.'

In the chapters which follow we will study critically not only the several components of the flowing action which prompted Arkwright to write so enthusiastically, but also such aspects of bird dog field trials as serve to make these competitions amongst the most exciting of all field sports. To assist the reader in his understanding of the text we include here a glossary of terms which are common to the hardened field trialler but may be unusual to the inexperienced enthusiast (Table 1).

Table 1   Field trial terminology

TERMS	MEANING
1. Backing	A dog acknowledges another dog's point by remaining motionless behind him.
2. Blinking the Point	A dog which can point, refuses to do so and moves away even though it knows game is nearby.
3. Boring	The dog moves directly forward into the wind.
4. Cast	To cast the dog is to start the dog hunting, usually to one side of the handler.
5. Cast Backward	After the cast the dog turns away from the oncoming wind.
6. Cast Forward	After the cast the dog turns forward into the oncoming wind.
7. Chapping the Point	The dog on point appears to be munching something and is slavering.
8. Down Position	The dog lies flat but alert, with its belly and four legs close to the ground.
9. Drawing	The dog moves forward slowly in a pointing attitude, prior to remaining motionless, on point.
10. Drop to Wing or Shot	The dog lies down whenever game flies up or a shot is fired.
11. False Point	The dog assumes a pointing stance when there is no scent of game before him.

TERMS	MEANING
12. Feathering	The dog reduces its speed, and in a semi-crouching attitude takes short excited casts often with much tail wagging, as if expecting to find game nearby.
13. Flush	Disturbing birds by running into them without pointing.
14. Giving Tongue	Yelping or barking while quartering.
15. Haunt	A place where animals visit frequently, usually to feed.
16. Leaving the Point	A dog on point, distracted by some other interest, moves away from the game.
17. Lining	The dog, with nose to the ground, follows a foot scent, usually in a straight line.
18. Losing the Point	The dog cannot maintain its point because of a change in scenting conditions.
19. Making out the Covey	The dog, after roading in to raise birds, ensures none of the covey remains in hiding.
20. Non-productive Point	A dog gives every indication of the presence of game but no birds are found when the search is made.
21. Pegged	The handler, usually, is penalized.
22. Point	On point, the dog is motionless, indicating the presence of nearby game.
23. Pottering	The dog works ineffectually with neither zest nor pace.
24. Pulling	Tending to cast too widely despite the handler's commands.
25. Quartering	The dog passes to and fro across the path of the handler, hunting evenly on both sides by scenting the wind.

TERMS	MEANING
26. Raking	Hunting with the nose too close to the ground.
27. Roading	To walk the dog forward, under command, from a pointing position towards the game.
28. Stealing the Point	The dog fails to back, but advances to point in front of a dog already on point.
29. Sticky on Point	The dog refuses to road in when commanded to do so, or is extremely hesitant to move forward.
30. Turning In	Though quartering normally to and fro, the dog turns away from the on-coming wind at the end of each natural side cast, thus losing scent momentarily and starting his return cast on that part of the ground over which he has already hunted.

2 · SOME FUNDAMENTALS

No matter how lovable are the ways of bird dogs, no matter how knowing their looks and how sagacious their eyes, they are creatures of limited intelligence. Their natural will to please is based on a very limited understanding of rewards and retributions, of pleasures and pains. Bird dogs are neither conversationalists nor philosophers and have no knowledge of English grammar.

The initial commands offered to a bird dog should be simple, direct and as distinctive as possible. The dog must learn from an early stage that one command demands one reaction; one sound demands one reaction; one gesture demands one reaction. If, as sometimes happens, a compound instruction is used by the trainer, such as a command plus a gesture, he would be well advised to reduce the complexity of the instruction to a minimum, keeping all his commands as short and as distinguishable from one another as possible, and all his gestures simple, clear and decisive. Arkwright (ibid.) points out, in a quotation taken from *The Gentleman's Recreation* (1686),

'You must be very constant to the words of Direction by which you teach him, chusing such as are most pertinent to the purpose, and those words that you first use do not alter, for dogs take notice of the *sound* not of the *English*, so that the least alteration puts him to a stand. For example, if you teach him to couch at the word "couch" and afterwards will have him couch at the word "down", this will be an unknown word unto him; and I am of the opinion that to use more words than what is necessary for one and the same thing is to over load his memory and cause forgetfulness in him.' (P. 155.)

Note the stress which is laid here on the fact that the sound of the command is more important to the dog than any meaning the word may have in English. Note also the simplicity of the direction 'down'. To a dog working keenly in the field the sound it hears first will be the most meaningful of all the words the handler utters. Dispense, therefore, with the rudiments of grammar and do not baffle with needless verbs one who cares nothing for the nuances of English. If the command is 'down', 'drop', or 'flat', say not 'get down', 'please drop', or 'lie flat', it merely confuses the issue.

While on this topic it is well to recognize how readily a dog will respond to the *tone* of his handler's voice. Thus 'good dog' spoken in pleasing tones will communicate to him more of your pleasure than long sentences extolling his virtues. Conversely, 'bad, bad dog' said in harsh tones will strike him more deeply than curses and well turned epithets. Dogs are not students of phraseology. They take their joy from the *sound* of the handler's pleasure and their unhappiness from the *sound* of his anger.

From what has been said it will be evident to the reader that in some particulars a whistle may have advantages over the voice. Not only does its sound carry farther against the wind, but its constant pitch is passionless. Many a handler, despite his best efforts, finds it impossible when provoked by a dog's mistakes, to keep some tone of irritation from his voice. This, when communicated to the dog, often serves only to aggravate his errors. The use of a whistle therefore is imperative for most field triallers, and, though it is true a dog can be confused when, by chance, two handlers use whistles of similar pitch, experience quickly teaches a dog that the manner in which his particular whistle is blown is quite distinctive.

Of the handler himself it has been written

'the chief requisites in a breaker are—firstly, command of temper, that he may never be betrayed into giving one unnecessary blow; secondly, consistency, that in the exhilaration of his spirits, or in his eagerness to receive a bird, he may not permit a fault to pass *unreproved* (I do not say unpunished) which at a less exciting moment he would have noticed—and that, on the other hand, he may not correct a dog more harshly because the shot has been missed, or the game lost; and lastly, the exercise of a little reflection, to enable him to judge what meaning an unreasoning animal is likely to attach to every word and sign,—nay to every look.'[1]

To this advice, so clearly expressed by the late General Hutchinson, may be added the view that no trait is more desirable in a trainer than an ability to appreciate the temperament of his dog. Accurately assessed, it will direct both the order and the methods of training to be used, and will help the handler to develop to its highest pitch the latent talent of his charge.

[1] Hutchinson, W. N., *Dog Breaking*, 10th ed. (London: John Murray, 1898), p. xv.

3 · NATURAL FRIENDS AND ENEMIES

The bird dog has no greater natural friend than the wind for it carries towards him the body-scent of game. The best trainers are continually conscious of the direction of the wind and utilize it during work to give their dog every advantage. Experienced field triallers or judges can be seen lifting their faces to the sky in order to feel for the direction of the wind, in much the same way as their bird dogs raise sensitive nostrils to sniff the air for scent.

Cheek wind
(i.e. a side wind)

Upwind
(i.e. a head-on wind)

Downwind
(i.e. a following wind)

Diag. 1 Description of the wind's direction when a dog is running

In Diagram 1 we show some of the terms used to describe the wind's direction. A gentle and steady breeze blowing towards the dog is of the most value to him. Strong gusts bring the scent only in tantalizing but discontinuous whiffs. The terms shown refer only to the wind's overall direction and tell nothing of the state of the wind about ground level. The nature of the wind at the height of the dog's nose is all important. Often, the breeze the handler feels against his face is similar to that reaching the dog; but not always. Therefore, to estimate correctly both the direction of the wind and its force, at the level of the dog's head, handlers may study the effect of the wind upon a handkerchief held by two corners at knee level, or watch carefully the fall of a few blades of grass released from the hand, or follow the drift of smoke from their cigarettes and pipes, or the vapour of their breath.

Experience quickly teaches the novice handler that the wind may be altered locally by walls, hedges, banks of trees, and even the natural curves of the terrain. Under the lee-side of a wall or hedge, for example, there is usually little or no wind. What breeze there is may circulate into small whirlwinds or blow in irregular eddying patterns (Diagram 2). It is so easy to be misled about the state of the wind below a wall when, in the face of the handler, a fresh and steady breeze blows over it. How carefully must he watch his dog, running beneath a seemingly innocent woodland or hedge. How keenly must he await the first back-cast, that first sure sign the dog seeks a more favourable wind. If this turn, an effort to recapture the breeze, remains unnoticed, and the dog is encouraged to advance towards a windless void, grave risks await him of casting unexpectedly into a sheltering covey of birds. More field trials than one have been lost by such an error. Anticipation is

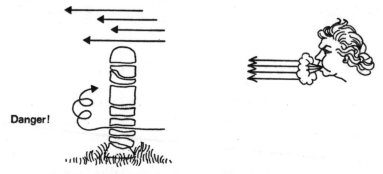

Danger!

Diag. 2 *The danger of a wall*
The wind curls and eddies on the sheltered side

the remedy. Prior to entering the windless zone, let the handler drop his dog. Then, should the judge prefer him to continue the run he may indicate his wish to the handler. Meanwhile the handler's caution may well have prevented a disqualifying flush.

An unexpected and sometimes hazardous situation can exist when natural terrain is shaped like a bowl. At the rim the wind may be strong and steady but, as the dog runs down the slope, drawing towards the base of the bowl, the wind begins to blow over his head and the scent is lost (Diagram 3). Unwarily, the dog draws too near to his birds and they are flushed. Had he been stopped when drawing, the handler might have claimed his point and followed by confidently advancing his dog to raise the covey.

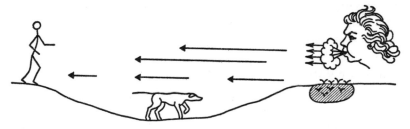

Diag. 3 The wind blows over a dog in a hollow
As he loses the scent he may draw forward uncertainly

Few temptations are so irresistible to the bird dog as a running hare or rabbit. Consciousness of the sin they commit in no way diminishes a dog's excitement of the chase, and retribution is as nothing compared with the exhilaration of the moment. 'Live now, pay later' becomes their motto. Beware the hare. Beware the scent line he leaves. So pungent is his aroma that few dogs will cross his path without pointing, or following swiftly the line of his recent departure, their ears stopped to all recriminations and their nose applied resolutely to the ground.

Equally tantalizing may be those silly sheep which gambol before a dog, shaking their woolly coats in his face. Flocking in all directions at once they provide irritating hazards to every handler. No dog, however, may be forgiven the misdemeanour of sheep-chasing. Understandable though the provocation may be, dogs must be taught the error of such ways. Often, sheep-chasing is a mark of inexperience in bird dogs. Those whose mind is on their true purpose seem to have little interest in such frivolities. Thus, if the trainer can delay the dog's introduction to free-roaming sheep until the business of hunting birds has been well learned, it is often possible to avoid sheep problems altogether. The same is true for hares and rabbits, but their presence in the field is, of course, much less predictable. Let the trainer miss no opportunity to *lead* his dog between sheep, scolding him if he so much as glances in their direction. Never let him run freely in the vicinity of sheep until his training is advanced; even then, retain the strictest control, permitting him to roam no further than the distance within which you know you may handle him. At first, this may necessitate the use of a long line attached to the dog with which to check him if he shows a natural inclination to chase. Gradually, as he becomes more absorbed by his real work, he will ignore the sheep more and more until, eventually, strict control becomes unnecessary. If, despite his training, a dog cannot be prevented from chasing sheep he should not be worked.

Few people are fortunate enough to have a pen containing rabbits in which a dog may be taught his field manners. Moreover, a dog is quick to recognize the difference between wild and partially tame rabbits, so, whereas he may be on his best behaviour in the artificial environment of the pen, in the natural environment of the field or moor, where this long-eared enemy is a more tempting proposition, manners may be forgotten.

Needless to say, field trial judges will eliminate any dog which chases 'fur or feather'.

4 · GENERAL TRAINING

It has been clearly stated that the temperament of a dog should direct the order and methods of its training. To this we add that no training should be undertaken unless the handler wishes to do it. A training session should be a pleasure for handler and dog alike. If it is a chore for the trainer it will soon become one for his dog also.

Most handlers begin serious training only when their puppy is about six months old. Instruction may have to be withheld until a later time for some immature animals, but other dogs will accept, even press, for training before this.

A diffident dog may need initial encouragement. A bold dog may need to be suppressed. Whatever the animal's temperament, whenever training begins, more will be achieved by making games of the lessons than dull and routine disciplines. Lessons, therefore, should be kept alive, interesting, and quite short, say fifteen to thirty minutes.

Anticipate and avoid mistakes. Do not have to correct them. At first, teach each puppy individually. Only when the most important schooling has been completed is it wise to run a puppy with a companion. To run a youngster with an older dog before the puppy is self-sufficient may teach it only to watch and mimic its senior companion. Thereafter it may always prefer to follow and imitate another rather than hunt for itself.

Commence the initial lessons in a quiet setting where interruptions are unlikely. If early training is not perfected in an empty and secluded garden or paddock, disastrous disobedience may result later, when the dog is first introduced into an environment teeming with game. Even when training has advanced sufficiently to introduce the young dog to a field abounding with tantalizing new scents, first ensure, by carefully walking about the place, that no rabbits lie in hiding to tempt him when the leash is slipped. Seek to tackle the hare only when training is quite advanced.

Early lessons

Lessons which all puppies may learn initially include the meaning of the word 'no', which should be said sharply and firmly but not necessarily loudly, and accompanied by a determined admonitory shake using the scruff of his neck. If purposefully undertaken, without undue roughness, a young dog will quickly learn to respect the shake and harsh tone of the handler's voice and to prefer the warmth of 'good puppy' accompanied by a playful caress.

By repetition a puppy soon learns his name, especially if, when called, it happens to be feed time. Thereafter, many dogs keen to please will look at their trainer frequently, for instruction or praise. These moments should not be allowed to pass unnoticed or the dog, not unnaturally, will lose interest in his trainer and cease to pay him much attention.

Another simple lesson which can be started at an early age is the command to enter the kennel, or sleeping quarters. The order 'box' is useful for this. Young dogs, who need plenty of sleep, will readily accept this order if it is used at the appropriate time. Later on it can be used to direct dogs into a kennel or the car.

To encourage confidence in young dogs, especially those reared mainly in kennels, simple walks to and from a local shopping centre are often helpful. They learn at an early stage not to fear unusual noises, or other animals and people. Undue pulling on the lead should, of course, be checked, but for most young bird dogs it is equally inadvisable to insist on them walking to heel. The purpose of the walking exercise is to avoid nervousness, not to suppress interest and initiative.

Introducing a dog to his place in the car is a useful early

lesson. To begin with, the car is stationary, and later kept stationary but with the motor idling. After a while, a *short* journey may be tried. As the dog's nervousness subsides these journeys may be increased. Obviously, it is unwise to feed a dog before the journey, but afterwards he will eat his meal with relish.

When the puppy has become familiar with all the above routines, training may proceed a little further.

Timid puppies should not be suppressed further by unnecessary insistence on a 'down' command in early training. This may be delayed safely until their confidence and hunting ability has been established. By contrast a bold puppy may well benefit from learning to adopt the lying position at a command such as 'down', 'hep', 'drop', 'flat', or 'sss' spoken as a hissing sound. Choose one sound or word, keep it simple, and always be consistent, so as not to confuse the animal with unnecessary and meaningless conversation. Furthermore, never use the command unless you can insist upon it being promptly obeyed every time.

Never misuse the command 'down', always try to make it a means to an end, rather than an end in itself. Thus, at first, call the dog to you, give the order 'down', gently push the dog into the down position, and then either feed it, praise it or play with it. Let the 'down' position be maintained only for very short intervals at first. As the dog learns not to fear the position it may be maintained slightly longer.

Restlessness in the down position denotes uncertainty, or youthful forgetfulness. Sometimes the handler's right arm, if raised and maintained like a policeman halting traffic, helps to avoid such confusion in the watching puppy. Gradually he will associate the command with the arm signal and will adopt the 'down' position for either order or both.

One advantage of teaching a puppy the 'down' position in early training is that, subsequently it facilitates teaching of both the 'stay' command and the 'recall'. Thus, having given the order 'down' the dog will lie at the handler's feet. The command 'stay' is given, and then the handler takes *one short step back-*

wards, setting off with the foot farthest from the dog. After a few moments the handler moves forward again to rejoin the dog and praise him. On another occasion the same lesson may be repeated and, if successful, developed to include one step forward also. On no account should the dog be permitted to crawl forward on its belly to reach the handler. As the dog realizes his handler is neither to leave him for long nor move far away, he relaxes and is content to remain in the 'down-stay' position, alert and awaiting praise. He should not be disappointed.

Step by step, increasing the distance very gradually, the handler will eventually be able to move up to ten or fifteen paces from the dog, or walk slowly around him in a circle, or even roll a fur dummy into the area without enticing him to leave the 'down-stay' position. Thereafter, the dog may be ordered into the 'down' position to await for food at mealtimes. When the food is put before him he is ordered to 'stay'. To begin, the 'stay' position should be maintained only a moment or two before praising the dog and releasing him to eat. Temptation may prove irresistible at first but, by gentle insistence, the handler can quickly teach the dog that food will be obtained more speedily by obedience than disobedience. No attempt should be made to rush this aspect of training. Both handler and dog must establish mutual trust, and this endeavour should not be spoiled by haste.

To secure a quick and enthusiastic recall the handler may begin by leaving his dog in the 'down-stay' position and move forward about five paces. A light check-cord should be attached to the dog who, by this time, will be expecting the handler to return to praise him. Bending or kneeling down the handler now calls the puppy's name and gently tugs the cord, encouraging the dog to come to him. Repetition will soon teach the dog that when called he moves up for praise. Conversely, if not called he remains in the 'down-stay' position until praise is brought to him.

Once the above lesson is learned, so that without a check-cord the dog will come directly to the handler over a distance of ten or fifteen paces, the following development is easy.

Plate 1 *An English pointer on point*
This photograph is reproduced from *The Kennel Gazette* by kind permission of the Editor, and the photographer, Sally Anne Thompson

Plate 2 *An Irish setter on point*
From a photograph in *The Field* by kind permission of J. Tarlton, A.I.B.P., A.R.P.S., the photographer, and Mr. Wilson Stephens, Editor

Plate 3 An English setter on point
Photograph: *The Field*
Reproduced here by kind permission of the Editor of
The Kennel Gazette

Plate 4 A Gordon setter working in woods
This photograph was taken by Sally Anne Thompson

Taking the dog to a small, quiet and empty field, he may be allowed off the lead for a romp. As, from time to time, he passes near the handler a firm and commanding recall should be given. At the same time the handler turns and runs away from the dog who, expecting high jinks, will usually follow him. As the dog comes in the handler stands to receive and praise him, provides a quick caress and immediately releases him for a further run. Awaiting then the next moment when the dog's attention is voluntarily given, the handler repeats the recall procedure, offers praise when the dog returns and again encourages another romp. This routine is repeated several times. Soon the recall becomes associated in the dog's mind with a quick return for praise and a further gallop. When on the fifth or sixth occasion the lead is gently slipped over his head the dog takes no umbrage. A quiet walk home to regain his breath seems welcome.

So often inexperienced trainers ruin a recall lesson by curbing the dog's freedom the first time it returns. No dog who yearns to run will welcome such unwarranted and early restriction. Given a second chance to be free he is unlikely to renounce it until good and ready!

One warning: while allowing the puppy freedom to romp playfully, he should not be permitted to escape from the handler's sight, perhaps to discover game accidently. At this stage of development his youthful attempts to point, if unheeded by the handler, may result in game being raised unexpectedly and an unwholesome chase.

It will take several months of training to teach a young bird dog the preliminary lessons outlined so far. Some of the exercises, however, may be taught concurrently with the more specific bird dog training discussed in future chapters.

Advanced lessons

Because it is convenient to deal with general training altogether, several general lessons of an advanced nature will now be mentioned. It must be emphasized, however, that they are

c

only taught after the trainee is quite advanced, in many instances after the dog has learned the art of hunting. To introduce them earlier in the dog's training may be to court disaster.

The advantages of a whistle have been mentioned earlier. Assuming the dog has become familiar, really familiar, with the command and signal for 'down', a whistle signal may be introduced to promote the same response. Usually, one single blast is all that is required. A melody is unnecessary.

To begin, the dog should be attached to a long check-cord to keep him within hailing distance. The whistle is blown and followed immediately by the arm signal plus the verbal command for 'down'. If this is not obeyed the order may be reinforced by a quick tug on the check-line. As soon as the dog lies down, the handler goes to him with praise. It is unwise to allow the dog to rise until the handler has reached him. At first the dog may be a little confused by the whistle and check-cord. However, as his understanding enlarges he will appreciate the handler's aim, and with repetition will immediately adopt the down position in response to the whistle and arm signal. Verbal orders become unnecessary. The lesson may be repeated in time with a slightly wider gap between the handler and the dog until, at last, even when running freely at a distance, the dog will respond to the whistle by dropping at once. Whatever temptation may come before him, no dog should rise from the 'down' position before receiving permission to do so. Even in the later stages of training the handler always goes to the dog, not vice versa.

A separate whistle signal, often with a different tone, is employed by many trainers for the recall. The sound used most often is a series of quick 'peeps' even spaced. As the dog has already learned the nature of the verbal recall he may be allowed to run freely as described previously until called by name and commanded to 'come in'. During his return the whistle recall is given and soon the dog learns to associate the sound with a prompt return for praise. At this stage the trainer may try the effect of the whistle alone, especially when the dog is beyond hailing distance.

Teaching bird dogs to walk 'to heel' is not essential for their work. Indeed, if enforced too soon, rigid 'heel' discipline can inhibit a bird dog's natural will to run freely. There is no reason why bird dogs should not learn to walk to heel as retrievers do, but let the trainer take care not to spend undue time and effort on an exercise which does little to forward the bird dog's true purpose. By their nature most bird dogs are restless creatures, especially in the field. At trials many of them are inclined to pull hard against the lead. Such uncontrollable straining is tiring for both handler and dog and should be checked firmly with a sharp and determined command of 'No', supplemented by a quick backward snatch of the lead's slip-collar or an unexpected flick of the dog's hindquarters with the lead's handle. (One or two fern-leaves sometimes provide a light but useful switch for this purpose.) Dogs must learn they cannot progress any faster than their handler simply because they walk in front of him.

Bird dogs, when fully trained, must be steady to gun-fire. However, they are not introduced to shot until the end of their basic training. Young dogs may be cowed by gun-fire, or indeed any loud noise including shouting. When they have learned confidence, when they understand the nature of their work, when their interest and keenness is fully aroused, above all when they trust their handler, then may the shot be introduced. At first, the dog should be remote from the site of the shot: for example, in the 'down' position perhaps, at the opposite side of a field. His interest will be aroused by the noise. The handler, therefore, should carry the gun towards him, praise him for remaining steady, and let him investigate the gun. When it appears the new sound promotes no restlessness or fear, a shot may be fired as the dog is running freely at a distance. When he looks towards the handler the signal for 'down' may be given. In time, the gun is fired a little nearer to the dog, and the handler must be observant to judge the correct distance. Each shot should be accompanied by a signal for the down position. Ultimately, when walking together the handler, having prepared the dog by indicating in an exaggerated manner his intention to shoot at some mythical bird, may fire a shot over the dog. Being an expected and familiar noise the dog should now be unafraid. Perhaps he will voluntarily assume the 'down' attitude. Even if he does not, on such an occasion he should be praised and made to feel mighty pleased with himself.

Never repeat a successful exercise

One piece of advice which relates to all that has gone before regarding training has been left until the last. Under no circumstances should a handler be tempted to repeat an exercise successfully completed, simply to prove to himself it was no 'fluke'. Having known clearly what lesson he wished to teach, having taught it and achieved one successful response, leave the encore for another day. The second attempt may appear purposeless to the dog. In his confusion, or perhaps even through boredom, he may play the fool, especially if youthful. His disobedience will prove irritating to the handler who must either leave the lesson as a failure, rate his dog for being awkward, or insist upon yet another attempt to correct 'the fault'. How much better it would have been, would it not, to finish the lesson successfully and with a note of well-earned praise.

The handler's maxim

Avoid confusion
Avoid boredom
Avoid tiredness
Avoid mistakes

5 · GROUND TREATMENT

In field trial parlance 'ground treatment' means the manner in which a bird dog searches an area the hunter wishes to explore. No attribute of the bird dog should be more highly prized than meticulous ground treatment. Dogs which race from one point to another, intuitively so to speak, appear good to the untutored eye of an onlooker, but he does not see the game left behind. A dog which systematically searches every area of ground will find not only the birds discovered by its flashy companion, but also, perhaps, numerous other birds tucked away, hidden from all but the keenest search.

Ground treatment necessitates an understanding of at least three separate movements: 'quartering', 'the turn' and 'the cast', the last two being part of quartering.

Quartering

The bird dog's purpose in quartering is to search with pace and style every area of the beat systematically, keeping within a reasonable distance of the handler and leaving no game undetected. The best pattern to aspire after is shown diagrammatically in Diagram 4.

'Doubtless there is not one thing—I was going to say that there are no dozen things—in the whole art of dog-breaking which are so difficult to attain, or which exact so much labour as a high well-confirmed systematic range. Nature will not assist you—you must do it all yourself; but in recompense there is nothing so advantageous when it is at length acquired. It will abundantly repay months of persevering exertion. It constitutes the grand criterion of true excellence. Its attainment makes a dog of inferior nose and action far superior to one of much greater qualifications who may be tomfooling about, galloping backwards and forwards sometimes over identically the same ground, quite uselessly exerting his travelling powers; now and then, indeed, arrested by the suspicion of a haunt, which he is not experienced enough, or sufficiently taught, to turn to good account; and occasionally brought to a stiff point on birds accidentally found right under his nose. It is undeniable, *caeteris paribus*, that the dog who hunts his ground most according to the rule must in the end find most game.' (Hutchinson, ibid., p. xxix.)

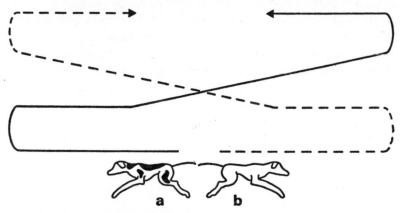

Diag. 4 Dog A ranges along the black line while dog B runs along the other (After Arkwright, p. 175)

When, at about the age of six months, a puppy shows signs of using his nose to recognize people or articles; when he demonstrates a desire to investigate unusual scents; in short, when he displays every evidence of a desire to hunt, lessons on quartering may begin. At first, lessons should be curtailed to ten or fifteen minutes until the puppy is well grown and physically fit. Even in more advanced training it should be remembered that during the time taken for a man to advance five or six yards a fast dog will move forty to fifty yards laterally. Thus, for every 150 yards walked by the trainer his puppy may have to run almost one mile, and prolonged training at such a pace will soon rob a dog of his merry and zestful style.

A strong but fine check-cord approximately 25 yards long and attached to a slip-lead, correctly applied (Diagram 5), is helpful in preliminary lessons. (A pair of leather gloves will prevent a painful friction burn should the check-line pass rapidly through the handler's fingers.) The training ground should be short heather, grass or stubble at least six to eight inches high. If the cover is longer the dog may tend to jump over it rather than run through it. If it is shorter he may tend to put his nose to the ground.

Diag. 5 The correct way to apply a slip-lead
(a) Front view (b) Side view

Upwind

Facing the oncoming breeze the handler leads his dog, on a fairly short lead, diagonally across the face of the wind. After a few paces a double 'peep' is blown on the whistle and the dog is guided into the wind, and brought diagonally across the original path to an equal distance on the other side. After two further 'peeps' the trainer once again turns the dog into the wind and brings him diagonally back again across the path. The whole process is repeated until it appears the dog has learned that a double sound of the whistle is to be followed by a fairly sharp turn about, always facing into the wind.

The pattern can now be repeated with the dog being given more freedom on the check-line and encouraged to trot. As he crosses before the handler, the check-line is flicked across the dog's back to the windward side and the handler steps forward so that, following the whistle signal, the dog may be guided

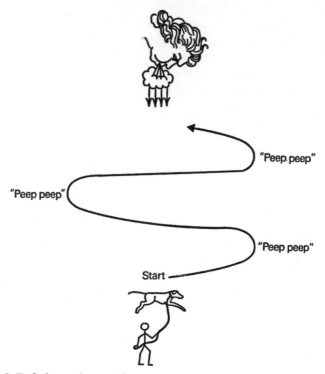

Diag. 6 Early lessons in quartering
At each 'peep peep' of the whistle the dog is turned with the check-cord

into the wind and turned back across the mid-line (Diagram 6).

As the dog's confidence and pace increase the handler will need not only to flick the check-cord quickly across the dog's back, but also endeavour to move forward several paces to get in front of the dog's beat. There, after blowing the turn signal he will need to move promptly in the direction of the dog so that the slip-lead tightens only gradually about the neck, gently but firmly slowing the dog and turning him into the wind without any sudden or frightening jerks (Diagram 7).

This exercise should be practised, perhaps with a slightly longer check-cord, until the dog will successfully maintain his quartering pattern over an area consistent with a spaniel-beat

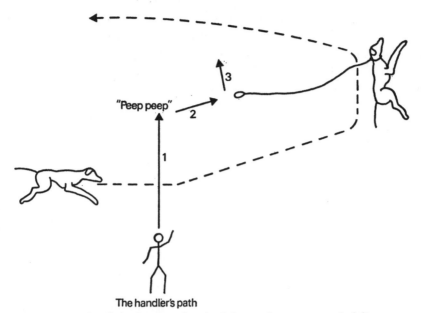

Diag. 7 The handler's direction when the dog's pace increases on a check line
To prevent a sudden jerk on the line the handler moves towards
the dog after whistling

(approximately twenty to thirty yards to right and left). Thereafter the pace should be increased and the beat widened
gradually until the limits of the line are reached. Subsequently
the cord should be released and allowed to trail freely. (At this
stage some handlers prefer to substitute a dog-harness for the
slip-lead to avoid a sudden and unwarranted jerk on the neck
if the check-cord should, inadvertently, catch in a stone or
crevice.) As Hutchinson (ibid.) put it, so admirably,

'Though you may be in an enclosed country, let him range
at first from no more than seventy to eighty yards on each
side of you. You can gradually extend these lateral beats as
he becomes conversant with his business—indeed, at the
commencement rather diminish than increase the distances
just named, both for the length of the parallels and the space
between them. Do not allow the alluring title "a fine wide
ranger" to tempt you to let him out of leading-strings. If he

be once permitted to imagine that he has a discretionary power respecting the best places to hunt, and the direction and length of his beats, you will find it extremly difficult to get him again well in hand. On the moors his range must be far greater than on the stubbles, but still the rudiments must be taught on this contracted scale, or you will never get him to look to you for orders' (p. xxviii).

With increasing confidence and pace, especially when the turn signal is obeyed without assistance from the check-cord, the handler may encourage even further speed by whistling for the turn while moving quickly away from the quartering dog (Diagram 8). Seeing his trainer apparently leaving him, the dog will tend to move faster to overtake. Meanwhile, the handler waves his near arm across his front as if pulling the dog across the mid-line, or else, with his offside arm, points in the direction he wishes the dog to travel. When this exercise has been successfully completed the slip-lead or harness may be removed. The dog's natural exuberance at receiving his freedom may, at first, drive from his memory some of the lessons so recently learned. The trainer should not be alarmed at this, but he should replace the check-line, shortening it before each lesson, progressively but imperceptibly, until about two yards only remain. Believing himself always under the handler's control, the dog will continue to range swiftly and evenly on either side of the handler, each time turning forward about six or eight yards, and hardly noticing the ever-diminishing resistance of the shorter and shorter cord trailing across the ground. At last, nothing but the slip-lead itself or the harness remains to be taken off, and these should be removed part-way through a lesson, when the quartering pattern for the day is firmly established in the dog's mind.

'As the powers of scent vary greatly in different dogs, the depth of their turns (or parallels), ought to vary also, and it will be hereafter for you to judge what distance between the parallels it is most advantageous for your youngster ultimately to adopt in his general hunting. . . . What you have to guard against is the possibility of their being so wide (*deep*) that birds may be passed by unnoticed.' (Hutchinson, ibid., p. xxix.)

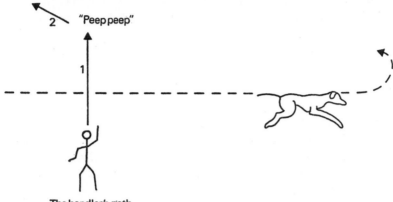

Diag. 8 *The handler's direction when the dog is quartering without a slip-lead*
After whistling the handler moves away from the dog

In field trials, where two dogs run at the same time, a dog's determination to achieve the forward cast first may significantly alter the distance of his natural sweep forward, i.e. the depth between his parallels. Some dogs are naturally 'front runners', and if two such dogs are matched their handlers may have extreme difficulty in preventing them both from taking sweeps forward which are too deep.

A more adventurous, if less certain method of teaching a dog to quarter provides an alternative to the techniques described above. In a field devoid of game, along which a fair breeze blows, the handler releases his dog, watching carefully to ensure he does not bore out into the wind but runs instinctively across the face of the breeze and to the side of the handler. At a distance which the handler deems suitable he attracts the dog's attention with the whistle. As soon as the dog looks towards him the trainer moves in the opposite direction encouraging the animal to run past him. A dog with a true instinct for quartering will then gallop back across the mid-line of the beat to continue onwards and hunt the other side. At the appropriate distance the handler again will whistle for a change of direction.

Using this method the trainer relies solely upon a dog's instinct for work. Little control of the dog can be exercised if he runs awry. For a natural worker, however, or perhaps for a timid dog which may be alarmed by slip-leads or check-cords, the method may prove valuable.

In teaching a puppy to quarter his ground it does not help to run him with an older, trained dog. Puppies are likely to follow or even chase their older companion and, if they cannot catch him, sometimes become excited enough to 'give tongue', a bad habit which it is difficult to eradicate.

Pace in quartering, although desirable, should be encouraged sensibly. There is an old adage which states 'the shorter his nose, the faster he goes', suggesting that pace varies inversely with an ability to scent birds. It is not wholly true. Moreover, when introduced to game the handler should watch his dog's progress very carefully. An aptitude to accommodate to the prevailing conditions should be encouraged in a dog. A certain caution, so long as it does not reduce a handsome pace to an ineffective pottering, is laudable. Allow the dog to regulate his pace according to the winds. Perhaps, if his nose is to the ground and he is 'raking'—a situation liable to finish with a flush—it is reasonable to demand a change in pace. For example, if the pace can be increased, the dog must raise his nose to run. If the pace cannot be increased it may be wiser to avoid a mistake and whistle the dog 'down'.

Turning away from the wind at the end of a beat is a problem commonly encountered. Interestingly enough a dog usually turns correctly on one side but incorrectly on the other. Indeed one field trialler raised the possibility that some dogs may be naturally 'right-handed', others 'left-handed', like humans. To correct 'turning in', or 'back casting' as it is sometimes called, the handler must first ensure he has stepped far enough forward after the quartering dog has passed him. From the advanced position the handler is satisfactorily placed to entice his dog forward at the turn. This technique, although suitable for training, can be undesirable when hunting for birds. Hutchinson (ibid.) describes the problem in the following manner:

'You may at first strive to correct your dog's turning too
abruptly inwards . . . by pushing on in your own person
further ahead on your own beat; but when he has acquired
if merely the slightest idea of a correct range, be most careful
not to get in advance of the ground he is to hunt. Your doing
so might habituate him to cross the field diagonally (thereby
leaving much of the sides of the fields unhunted), in order to
get ahead of you; and moreover, *you* might spring birds
which you are anxious he should find.' (P. xviii.)

Should this method of stepping forward prove either un-
successful or unsuitable, the handler may allow the back-cast to
occur but subsequently drop the dog as he approaches the mid-
line of the beat. Then, recasting him to the same side it will
often transpire that the dog undertakes a correct turn at the
end of his beat. Further alternative corrective measures are
possible with the help of a cheek wind.

Cheek wind

Emphasis has been placed upon the importance of working
young dogs into the wind. Great care should be taken about
this until they are well schooled. At that time, however, they
may, with advantage, be introduced to the problems of
quartering their ground with a 'cheek wind'. Commonly the
wind is only partially on the cheek as shown in Diagram 9,
consequently the dog slightly inclines the angle of his beat to
capture as much of the wind as possible. If he runs an equal
distance laterally on both sides of the beat, it is evident he will
run behind the handler on the side *from* which the wind blows.
This is undesirable, not only because he will then be working
behind the line of guns, incurring all the concomitant dangers
of such a position, but also because he cannot be handled
adequately behind the trainer. In practice, a well schooled dog
tends to cut short his beat on the windward side, and elongate
it on the opposite side as in Diagram 9. Should he fail to do so

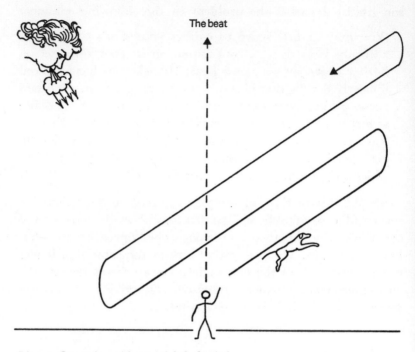

Diag. 9 Quartering with a partial cheek wind
To make maximum use of the wind the dog runs obliquely to the beat

naturally he may, of course, be turned by the handler's whistle.

A cheek wind can be most useful in helping to correct a dog who tends normally to quarter his ground unevenly on each side. By working him with the appropriate cheek wind he may learn to lengthen his beat on one side or the other (Diagram 10). Should this technique fail, uneven quartering can also be improved when working upwind, by taking the shorter beat as the dog's natural measure and turning him by whistle, or even stopping him, at an equal distance on the side of his longer beat. Once corrected, the dog will soon re-adjust to an equal and natural measure of his own on both sides.

If a dog's natural beat tends to be short, a cheek wind sometimes helps to increase his range. For example, by working the dog both up and down a beat which enjoys a cheek wind (Dia-

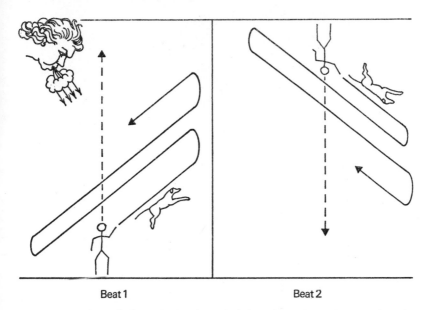

Beat 1   Beat 2

Diag. 10 Using a cheek wind to lengthen a dog's lateral cast. Beat 1 increases the right cast. Beat 2 increases the left cast

gram 10), it can be seen that the dog's range is increased first on the right side, and then on the left. (Incidentally, when utilized in field trials, a cheek wind of this type facilitates economical use of the ground, provides a good test for the dogs and saves the competitors a great deal of walking!) The more usual alternative, which is to work always directly into the wind, necessitates competitors returning to the starting line after every beat has been completed, then moving to right or left to begin the hunt on fresh ground (Diagram 11).

Yet another problem which a cheek wind may help to solve is that of 'turning in' on one side. By running the dog slightly downwind, or away from the cheek wind he may notice more readily that the scent of game is available to him only on one aspect. This is the direction towards which he will instinctively turn at the end of his beat. Thus, a dog which tends to turn in on the right should be worked with a cheek wind from the left, and vice versa.

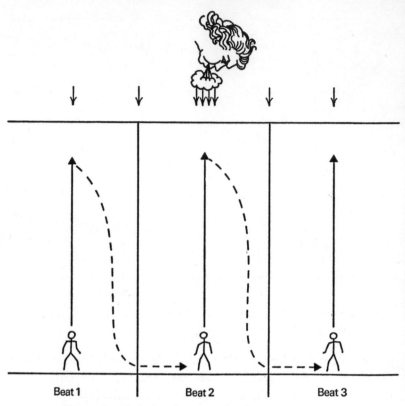

Diag. 11 The usual method of working ground in field trials
        After each beat the handler returns and moves across to another
        section

Downwind

A dog should not run downwind until he has considerable
experience of quartering into the wind, and possibly on a cheek
wind also. Before attempting to hunt downwind he must have
learned caution and obedience, and developed a certain 'game
sense'. Obviously when running with the wind there is a risk of
careering directly into unsuspected coveys. With young dogs
especially, this should always be avoided. An older and more
experienced dog soon realizes that by moving downwind it becomes possible to turn into the wind and quarter the ground

Plate 5 Pointers. Backing in a field
This photograph was taken by Sally Anne Thompson

Plate 6 Pointers. Backing on the moors

back towards his handler. Meanwhile the handler must wait patiently (Diagram 12). After the beat has been searched the dog may take a further cast downwind and once again begin to quarter fresh ground. Meanwhile the handler advances across the area his dog has just cleared.

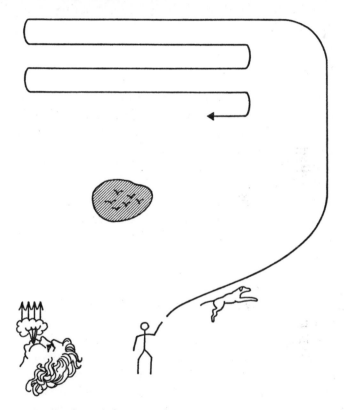

Diag. 12 Hunting downwind
The dog searches the ground by quartering towards the handler

For any handler to enter a beat which his dog has not searched is folly. Undetected coveys will be raised by walking into them. In field trials a dog, through no fault of his own, may be disqualified by such an error. When hunting downwind, all the ground ahead of the handler must be searched before he advances. As it takes time for the dog to accomplish this task,

D

the handler's forward progress must of necessity be correspondingly restrained. If the dog points, the handler joins him by moving widely around the covey. When shooting, it is true that the two or three guns are unlikely to move round the covey in this way. More commonly they will spread out in line and advance slowly towards the pointing dog, shooting at any birds they 'walk up'.

The cast

The purpose of the cast is to set the bird dog hunting. Sometimes it is accompanied by a command such as 'seek', or 'get on', though many bird dogs, in their keenness, require no such order to set them to work.

The cast is a dangerous moment. The dog is excited at the prospect of game. His attention is partly distracted by the nearness of the handler. He has not yet settled to the rhythm of his beat. He is unsure of the wind's direction and force. How easy it is for him to make a mistake when, with enthusiastic bounds, he leaps forward to establish the conditions of work. Before he gets the chance to settle to his task, a nearby covey may be alarmed and flushed.

It was related by one of the more senior field trial judges that prior to the 1939–45 war, competitors at field trials were expected to cast their dogs in opposite directions, one to the left, the other to the right. Today less insistence is put upon this and often both competing handlers cast their dog the same way. In fact such a cast can prove disastrous, especially with young dogs, for jealousy, bravado, or just simple playfulness may entice both of them to run unwisely or thoughtlessly. Their lack of concentration may then result in some mistake which disqualifies them both.

It is useful to accustom the dog to commence hunting on the side of the beat to which he is cast by his handler. If the wind is favourable this usually proves no difficulty. However, when the wind is in an unhelpful quarter the dog, as soon as he is released, is likely to look for the best wind conditions he can find, and it may be difficult, even unwise, to insist upon him running towards one specific side.

Should one of the two running dogs appear wild and uncontrolled at the cast, the handler of the other would be well advised to keep his dog, as one experienced field trialler put it, 'as close to the bosom as possible—close enough to spit on if need be'. In this fashion, work on the beat should continue until the judge calls it to a halt.

Boring out into a wind coming head on is likely to disqualify a dog. Under such conditions he is expected to quarter laterally. The handler must take care, therefore, if he suspects such a possibility, to cast his dog strictly to one side. By contrast, when the wind is on the cheek, the dog receives the greatest advantage from being cast with the wind. At the end of his beat, which is usually a wide one, he turns to receive the full benefit of the oncoming wind (Diagram 13). If cast the opposite way, i.e. directly into the cheek wind, he often takes a short cast initially and

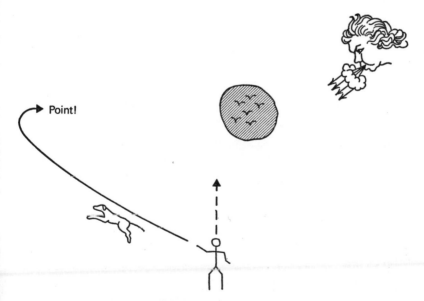

Diag. 13 *The advantage of casting with a cheek wind*
At the turn the dog receives the strong scent of birds

turns quickly, sometimes flushing birds nearby or even missing their scent altogether (Diagram 14).

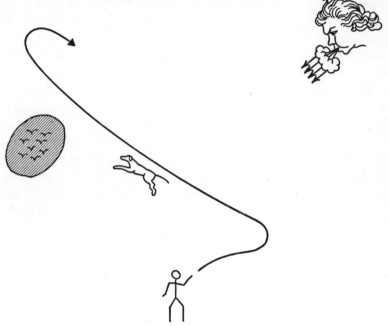

Diag. 14 Casting into the cheek wind
The dog turns because he scents no birds. Running 'downwind' he misses their scent again and flushes the covey or passes them unnoticed

It sometimes happens in field trials, as two competitors approach the judges, that their dogs behave in a manner which makes both handlers suspect the presence of game adjacent to the starting point. If, subsequently, perhaps in the hope of gaining a point before his fellow competitor, one handler is sufficiently unwise to cast his dog directly at the place he believes the birds to be, he is likely to suffer for his folly. In all probability the birds have run through the cover at the competitor's approach. The dog, in the excitement of the cast, completely misjudges their proximity and most frequently gallops straight into the middle of them, flushing birds in all directions. The handler would have been wiser had he cast away from the area he suspected, thus giving this dog a few moments to run off his exuberance, settle to his task, assess the wind, turn, in his own time, and approach the covey in full command of all his senses.

A similar situation occurs when competitors are asked to re-cast their dogs following a find. Usually, before casting, they all advance beyond the place of the recent point to prevent any remaining scents confusing the dogs. The handler who then fails to cast away from the area is likely to see his dog, especially if inexperienced, back-cast sharply, return to the scene fixed

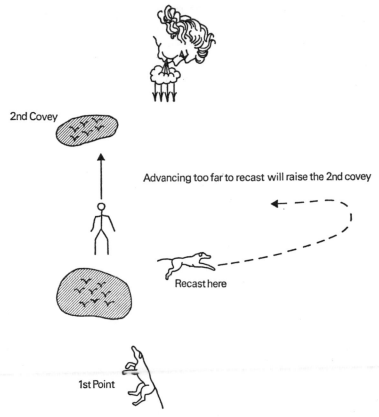

Diag. 15 *When game is plentiful do not advance too far to recast*

vividly in his memory, and there puzzle ineffectively over ground scent which is too fresh to be distinguished easily from the true presence of feeding birds. Had the cast been made away from the area it is likely this problem would not have arisen. The dog would have been so remote from the area at the end of his cast, he would have turned forward for new scents in preference to back-casting solely to renew acquaintances with old ones.

The only circumstance in which handlers do not recast their dogs well in advance of the raised covey is when game is so plentiful that coveys lie close together. For example, as shown in Diagram 15, if competitors and judges advance too far the second covey will take flight before the dogs can be set hunting. To walk far beyond the disturbed birds would only raise a third covey, and so on. In such unusual circumstances judges will probably direct handlers to recast their dogs just beyond the edge of the raised covey, thereby avoiding this dilemma.

6 · POINTING

The purpose of pointing is to indicate to the handler the position of game. The triad of pointing to the birds' scent, moving forward under control to raise the covey, then dropping to the ground as birds fly off, comprises the pattern of events by which a trained bird dog manages game. Although it is instinctive in most bird dogs to point whenever they locate the scent of fresh game, this instinct may be dormant in a puppy and have to be awakened by the handler.

'In practice the handler will learn much about scents and scenting at this stage by watching his dog's reactions and he will also learn much about his dog's capabilities and nose. The faint wag of the tail acknowledging the scent of a covey of partridges which departed as the handler entered the field, the brief check at a hare's form still warm with the imprint of the occupant, the drop of the head to examine a recent foot scent, and the raised head testing the air preparatory to the point, all these and many more signs tell their story to the observant handler as he watches his dog. He will find that it pays to watch his dog constantly and learn to interpret these signs correctly.'[1]

Many young bird dogs will point at the *sight* of game, indeed at the sight of any object they take to be of unusual interest, including sheep or boulders. Even experienced dogs will point by sight at a grouse covey with their heads all stretched above the heather, 'like candles' as one judge put it. Actually, pointing by sight is of no great value and, though it need not be

[1] Brander, M., *Gundogs, Their Care and Training* (London: A. & C. Black, 1963), p. 69.

actually discouraged, it is essential that a bird dog always points at the scent of game rather than at the sight of it.

In general, serious training to develop a dog's pointing ability should be delayed until the 'down' command and lessons in quartering are well established. A naturally occurring opportunity to point should never be neglected, and attempts to chase flying birds should always be chastised except, perhaps, for the first or second occasion on which a dog detects birds naturally and is investigating the significance of their scent.

It is not realistic to attempt to teach a young dog to point without a live bird to arouse his interest. Few trainers, however, have access to game just at the time their dog is ready for training. So either they concentrate on the dog's other lessons in the hope that he will point naturally when presented with game in the field, or else they find a substitute for game. Even when, by chance, game birds are available locally for training, there are problems about using them to teach a young dog to point. In the first instance the precise location of the covey is probably unknown. Much time may be wasted in finding the particular field where they reside. Secondly, the trainer cannot always arrange to be in control of his dog at the critical moment the covey is scented. Even when trailing a check-cord, it is surprising how often a dog may be just beyond the manageable distance from his handler. Then, should a mistake be made, should the covey be flushed, should the dog chase his birds despite the trainer's efforts to whistle him 'down', the whole purpose of the exercise is lost. Thirdly, if, to avoid the possibility of a mistake, the handler retains hold of the dog's check-cord, it is unlikely wild game will remain quietly by until both dog and man together approach near enough for a useful lesson to be taught.

Enthusiastic amateurs, including one of us (J.M.B.), have attempted to use various alternatives in place of game. Some of these are reported here if only to prevent others from pursuing similar misconceptions. One of the less helpful methods and, in retrospect, one of the more ludicrous was an idea obtained initially from a magazine.

'A pair of wings removed from a recently killed pheasant was attached to the end of a long fishing line and rod. The device having been left in suitable cover, I guided the setter towards the area on a check-cord in the hope he would be fascinated, first by the sight, and subsequently by the faint scent of the wings. I lifted the rod and made an attempt to "flutter" the lure at a distance. Not only was the dog more interested in the rod than the wings, but the scent left him totally unmoved. The check-cord and fishing line became entwined, the dog grew excited, the wings broke loose, blew towards him and he chewed them.'[1]

Another disappointment followed the use of hand-reared pheasants which were placed individually in light string bags and set down in a field.

'Having located them easily enough, the dog showed no inclination to point them but nudged them instead with his nose, passed water on each bird in turn and ran on. One pheasant, forgivably irate at such treatment, burst from the bag and flew off.' (J.M.B., ibid.)

Numerous handlers have noted that hand-reared pheasants recently released from pens appear to be of no interest to bird dogs, who treat them more as domestic fowls.

'It was my own salutary experience when invited to demonstrate the prowess of an experienced field trial dog to a group of interested onlookers, to release him in a field of semi-tame hand-reared pheasants, none of whom would he acknowledge and all of whom flew indiscriminately before his resolute gallop as he charged hither and thither, hunting for wild game.' (J.M.B., ibid.)

Early lessons

Perhaps the most practical bird to use in order to teach a dog to point is the ordinary homing pigeon. A small loft containing,

[1] From the personal notebook of J.M.B.

say, six homing pigeons will prove of inestimable value to the trainer.

When rocked gently to and fro in the hands, a pigeon becomes slightly dizzy and will remain quietly on the ground until it has regained its orientation. Handlers have utilized this phenomenon to train bird dogs to point. Bringing a dog on a check-cord near to the resting bird, they encourage the pointing stance and, as the bird flies home, drop the dog.

Certain drawbacks attend the method. In particular, it is not possible to estimate how long the bird will remain still. As it must be hidden from the dog, there is an inevitable time lapse between setting down the bird and collecting the dog. Frequently the bird has flown before the handler returns. Often it flies just prior to establishing the point. Sometimes it remains in place far longer than the trainer would wish, necessitating a prolonged point in an inexperienced dog. Lastly, the bird itself is unprotected from such unforeseen accidents as breaking of the check-cord. In our view the following method is undoubtedly preferable.

The birds may be placed gently into traps of the dimensions shown in Diagram 16 and set quietly in a field, the release cords being attached to convenient markers at a distance of approximately twenty yards. If the pigeons are left undisturbed for some twenty to thirty minutes the scent surrounding them becomes of considerable interest to young dogs. At all times the birds are safely protected and secure. Knowing their whereabouts precisely, the trainer may attach his dog to a check-cord, encourage limited quartering up to the marker and then, at the first sign of the dog receiving a whiff of scent, caution him with the command 'to-ho, to-ho' or 'steady, steady', while restraining him with the line. The dog may attempt to rush towards the hidden bird at first, but the handler must continue to hold him securely, stroking him gently along his back and tail, cautioning him all the while to be steady. As the dog becomes more certain of the scent, he will stiffen to a firm point. The cord may then be relaxed gradually, but taken in again if any attempt is made to move forward.

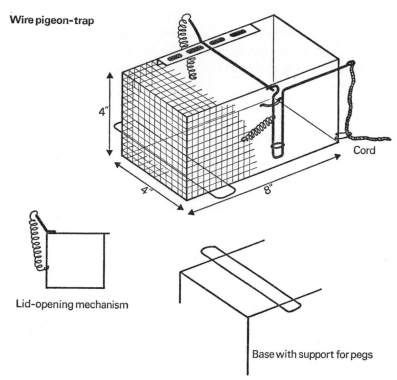

Wire pigeon-trap

4"

4"

8"

Cord

Lid-opening mechanism

Base with support for pegs

Diag. 16 An example of a pigeon-trap

Initially, the point should be held for just a few moments, after which, on the command 'move up', for example, the dog approaches nearer to the bird in a cautious manner. Then the trap is sprung and the bird released while still at a safe distance from the dog. As the pigeon rises the command 'down' is firmly given, and this position should be maintained by the dog until the bird is clear. Thereafter, with whatever restraint is necessary, he may be permitted to advance again, very cautiously, right up to the trap, there to investigate closely the warm scent and the surrounding ground. When his search is complete, praise him generously, let his attention be regained and lead him away under control. Any attempt to return to the site should be thwarted, and reinforced firmly but gently with the statement 'gone away'.

The lesson may have to be repeated several times in its simplest form before the dog recognizes its own natural aptitude for pointing. With practice, however, he should find no difficulty in ultimately maintaining a point for up to five minutes or more. When the time comes the handler may profitably lay out several traps in different parts of the field, sometimes placing two or more close together. Bringing the dog, under control, to the first, the point may be encouraged and subsequently the bird raised as just described. Thereafter, the dog may be brought to a second point which, when he is eventually allowed to move in, results in two or three birds being released at short intervals. Each pigeon in turn must be acknowledged by the dog assuming the 'down' position. Perhaps at a later lesson, when the point and release of pigeons have been successfully completed, it may be so arranged that a search about the trap enables him to scent an isolated bird hidden a short distance away.

These exercises, which mimic quite closely the experience a dog may receive in the field, should all be completed under controlled conditions before the dog is allowed to quarter freely and locate the pigeons for himself. However, when this state is reached, the trainer must take care not to use the same field for consecutive lessons, otherwise the dog when released may run straight to the place where he remembers the birds were found previously. If but one field is available let the birds be placed in different sites at each lesson so that the dog learns to quarter his ground afresh whenever he is set hunting.

Yet another use to which pigeons may be put is to teach the dog to drop if game flies by from an unexpected quarter. The trainer places a pigeon gently in the deep, wide pocket of his coat. During an episode of quartering, the pigeon is withdrawn carefully and released into the air as the dog passes nearby. At the same time the 'down' whistle is blown and the dog should lie flat. Any tendency to chase the rising bird must be quashed by a sound rating. Assuming the dog has learned his previous lessons adequately there is usually little difficulty in teaching him to acknowledge the unexpected bird.

Because pigeons can help to teach a dog to point, to raise birds, and to drop to wing, it must not be imagined there is no limit to their usefulness. With increasing wisdom and caution the dog hunting pigeons may begin to search not just for birds but for the marker to which the release cord of the trap is attached. Having located this he will then raise his nose to scent the birds, which he has come to know are always nearby. Moreover, if he realizes that his birds always escape when he moves forward from the point, he may develop an understandable reticence to advance when ordered to do so. At the first signs of these problems the undoubted usefulness of training on pigeons has come to an end. It is necessary now to progress to game.

Advanced lessons

Despite the lessons which have been assimilated so far a dog may still have much to learn when first introduced to game. Bird scents, for example, differ not only in their quality but also in their strength. Those arising from grouse are far stronger than those from pheasants, and partridges are said to be the weakest. Experience alone can teach a dog to differentiate one from another.

Skylarks which abound in many fields or moors can prove an irritating distraction to young bird dogs still unfamiliar with the scent of true game. These little birds, which poise or fly before them, encourage both chasing and disobedience. Only experience, coupled perhaps with an occasional reprimand, will serve to wean a dog from 'skylarking'.

Nothing should be more fascinating to the true bird dog than the scent of game. However, when trained only on pigeons released from traps at some artificial moment, a dog is likely to misjudge at first the distance from which to point wild game. Having caught a whiff of their scent he steadies himself and draws forward but does not stand off. Moreover, he commonly advances too far at first, flushing the birds. If possible, the handler should prevent such an accident by whistling down his

dog as it begins to draw forward. Should the error occur before
the dog is controlled the handler may be irritated with himself
but not with his dog. Learning the safe distance from which to
point each game bird without disturbing it is solely a matter of
experience. The handler must be patient. In particular he must
refrain from acting hastily.

> 'I need hardly warn you', says Hutchinson (ibid., p. xxix), 'to
> be careful not to interrupt him whenever he appears to be
> winding birds. However his nose may be by nature, it will
> not gain experience and discrimination unless you give him
> a certain time to determine for himself whether he has really
> touched upon a faint scent of birds, and whether they are in
> his front or rear, or gone away altogether. Like every other
> faculty his sense of smell will improve the more it is exer-
> cised.'

Pointing errors

Every tentative point a young dog makes should be treated
seriously by the handler, even when he suspects there is no
game ahead. Anything less can develop the error of 'leaving the
point'. Occasionally, a dog may do this anyway until certain of
the sensitivity of his nose, but the error can be easily corrected.
After sustaining a point for a few moments, the young dog who
tries to continue with his run should be speedily curtailed with
the 'down' whistle. A short and controlled investigation of the
suspicious area ensues which, when completed, is followed by
a cast as if a find had been made. Not infrequently game will be
present, indicating to the handler the need for additional experience before his dog is entered for trials.

'Leaving a point' should not be confused with the momentary pause of a cautious, experienced bird dog, so that he may
analyse more closely some unexpected whiff or air scent. Let
his circumspection be trusted and he will either continue
quartering or draw forward a little first to satisfy his curiosity.
When the uncertainty continues the handler may suspect a

hare scent, or perhaps a wily old cock-bird. In this case he would be wise to drop the dog and investigate the line as for a point, never letting the dog get too far ahead of him. If after about ten paces the dog continues to be uncertain, he may be recast.

Never let a young dog suspect his point is anything other than an important event. 'Leaving a point' may be understandable during a dog's early development, but allowed to pass unchecked it leads ultimately to a dog who is untrustworthy before game. In this context correction should not be taken to mean punishment. It is a grave error on the handler's part to punish a young dog for being uncertain of his point. The dog may then associate pointing with pain and recrimination. Thereafter, wishing only to avoid further chastisement, he will keep away from game whenever he recognizes it in the future, a fault called 'blinking the point'.

In field trials, the atmosphere of competition affects some dogs as much as their handlers. In particular, the nearer two dogs are to one another at the moment of the point the more difficult they are to control. Faults arise which may never occur when they are separated by a distance. A competitor whose co-handler's dog is on point should, initially, give his own dog the opportunity to acknowledge the point correctly, but should he neglect the opportunity the handler would be wise to whistle him down immediately.

Whereas a dog running singly may be content to make his point and await the arrival of the handler before advancing, when coupled with a brace-mate his attitude often differs. For example, two dogs arriving before a covey at the same moment may share the point. Not infrequently both, in their zeal to be first, vie with each other to get their nose fractionally ahead of their companion. In so doing they both creep forward alternately until the birds are flushed.

Should one dog point an instant before his companion, the second dog may choose to ignore the fact and advance to 'steal the point', an error which, needless to say, will result in his disqualification. If, instead, he chooses to behave correctly, taking his place immediately behind the pointing dog, the scent of game becomes so strong in his nostrils that he may be unable to allow the forward dog the sole joy of raising the covey. As the advanced dog is moved forward, manners are abandoned, and deaf to all forms of caution the rear dog follows or even overtakes his companion.

7 · ROADING

The purpose of 'roading', or moving forward from the point, is to raise hidden birds in such a way that they might be shot.

Preliminary pointing lessons will provide the basis of moving forward, but when that triad of events has been properly assimilated, particular attention can be paid to roading in.

It must be first ensured that the dog has no fear of the gun (cf. Advanced General Training, p. 35). Thereafter, lessons in pointing should be designed to include an occasional blank shot. If pigeons are utilized it is well to let the released bird become truly airborne before a blank is fired, to avoid unnecessary alarm. The dog, who will, of course, be occupying the 'down' position at this moment, is also less likely to be disturbed. When his attention is riveted on the bird, a verbal warning of the sudden noise to come will help to avoid frightening or surprising him. After the shot, let the trainer praise his dog and encourage further advance towards the sprung trap. As lessons progress the shot can be fired immediately after the 'down' command and, eventually, should replace it altogether. When the dog has gained confidence and learned to expect gunshot at the flight of birds, more than one shot can be fired. If the first blanks promote signs of anxiety the dog may be reassured, but the exercise should not be repeated until further experience has been gained with more distant gun-fire. A dog subjected to gun-fire when he lacks assurance about the gun cannot give his full attention to 'roading'. He may start with fright at the sound and, before the guns have reloaded, run forward several paces to flush the remainder of the covey. Steadiness to gunshot is as important in the bird dog as steadiness to 'fur' or 'feather'.

E

Nothing will associate the flight of the bird and gun-fire more firmly than shooting over a dog. This experience is not always easily gained however and, even when available, should be introduced carefully to young dogs. At field trials, for example, puppies are usually treated most considerately as they road in, no blanks being fired near enough to alarm them or encourage them to run in on raised birds.

Following a point the handler should get to his dog, especially a puppy, as quickly as possible to prevent him drawing towards the birds. Great care must be taken, however, not to approach the dog in undue haste, for this will cause him to look round at the trainer and break the point, or else precipitate him into roading forward prematurely, i.e. before the guns are aligned. Even when approached quietly many dogs will begin to road in as soon as their handler arrives within about six feet of them. At least one experienced field trialler, therefore, waits two to three yards behind his pointing dog until ordered by the judge to raise the covey.

The normal advance to raise a covey should be smooth and continuous. The handler should be near his dog, either alongside or a few feet behind so as not to hamper the aim of the guns. In field trials a position alongside the dog has the advantage of exercising more immediate control when there are hares or young birds (cheepers) about, or when coveys are disinclined to rise. Under such circumstances roading in may bring the dog within snapping distance of game. Birds flapping their wings in the dog's face as they rise, or bolting hares, may become irresistible. More than one dog has been left with a mouthful of tail feathers to indicate the error of his ways. By keeping close to the roading dog a handler is often able to prevent such an accident, either by ordering the dog 'down' at the critical moment, or by looking ahead to see the game and anticipate the problem.

Sometimes it happens that a dog can move forward until his nose rests against a bird so expertly camouflaged that its presence is undetectable by the handler without the closest scrutiny. Great care is necessary in dealing with this situation, for all but the most perfect dogs will grab at the bird if it so much as stirs. Officially, the dog should nudge the bird into flight, leaving it unmolested. Officially! At field trials, to prevent 'unpleasantness' judges will often permit the handler to raise such a bird himself. The handler then puts his hand very slowly between the dog and the bird and quickly scoops it up and away from the dog, giving the 'down' command at the same time. Naturally, there is less of a problem when the dog and the bird are separated by twelve inches or more. Either the handler or the judge can push the bird with their toe. Though the dog may disqualify himself by snapping he is unlikely to reach the object of his aim.

When two dogs have shared a point, or even if one dog has stolen a point, it is always the forward dog who roads in to the birds. As one field trialler put it, 'After a stolen point, he does the work and you get the marks'. To bring the rear dog forward is unfair to the advanced dog. Indeed, rarely will the first dog allow the second to pass in front of him. Usually he begins to road in also as the rear dog draws alongside. Jealously, both dogs then compete with one another to raise the birds, and the whole situation gets out of control.

Roading commonly results in a covey being raised simply and completely. However, in deep heather, or stubble containing corn heaps, single birds can tuck themselves away and easily escape detection. Old cock birds are particularly adept at running and hiding before ultimately doubling back on themselves to pass by the advancing dog. Incautious or hasty roading will end with a dog over-running a wily cock, but should an air scent be followed rather than the foot scent, the dog is likely to outwit the bird and, in field trials anyway, receive credit for his sagacity.

A non-productive point should not be confused with false pointing, which is the erratic and haphazard pointing of unimportant scents or objects. False pointing may be suspected if consecutive points bear little relation to a line, or the direction of the wind and roading in seems indefinite.

Many dogs will acknowledge the remaining scent of a

recently departed covey by a firm point and a purposeful advance towards a site covered with feathers or fresh bird-droppings. When the dog continues to advance, purposefully, but no signs of birds are seen, a 'non-productive' point must be suspected. In field trials the handler should trust his dog and continue roading in either until he is stopped by the judge, or until the dog recasts spontaneously because he has lost the trail.

When the wind is strong and the dog, with head held high, remains rigid, chapping his point as he roads in, birds are almost certainly ahead and the handler should continue resolutely. By contrast, when the dog's nose is to the ground, his advance uncertain, and the wind inconstant, it would be unwise to road him in more than twenty to thirty yards without looking to the judge for instruction. Taking judges sixty yards or more from the beat without ultimately being able to raise birds may well result in a dog being penalized.

If the dog, after roading in for a distance, recasts spontaneously, the handler should not expect to hunt his dog for more than a few yards to the right or left of the line. When the trail is lost, judges usually order both dogs to be cast again so that both have a chance to find if, indeed, there is game in the region.

Taking up a dog while he is truly roading in on point is both undesirable and unsatisfactory. The judges can neither penalize him nor give him credit. Moreover, when recast the dog is likely to excitedly race back to the area, flushing the birds as he does so.

When a dog is 'roading' he should approach game without hesitation, dropping only when it rises. It should be unnecessary for the handler to touch him, though puppies can sometimes be reassured by a gentle pat or stroke. Often, dogs getting close to game move forward only reluctantly, aware that a bold approach will precipitate their escape. When the hesitancy amounts to a partial or complete refusal to advance, called 'stickiness on point', the reticence has become a fault. To overcome the problem without touching the dog a handler may clear the ground immediately before him by stamping with his foot, or change to the opposite side of the dog, or even momentarily interrupt the scent by pushing a knee across the dog's nose, which has the effect of making the dog advance two steps around the handler's leg to recapture the scent. A judge would notice such tricks with some disfavour if they were used excessively.

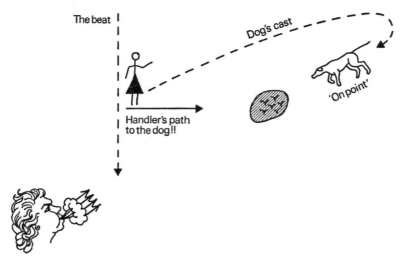

Diag. 17 An error in approaching a dog on point
The handler crossed unquartered ground and raised the birds prematurely

When the wind is on the cheek, or when hunting downwind, handlers must take care not to spoil a dog's point by inadvertently walking across the ground containing birds. Two examples will help to make this clear. In the first (Diagram 17), with the wind mainly on the right cheek, a dog who had worked brilliantly all day took a long cast, drawing to the left and scenting birds on the turn. The handler, unthinkingly, did not follow the same path but moved directly towards her dog across unquartered heather, thus scattering grouse which, correctly, should have been raised by roading in the dog. Needless to say, this momentary error by the handler lost her the stake.

The second example is depicted in Diagram 18. Working downwind in a narrow field of stubble, the dog took a long downwind cast, and turned to a point facing the handler. After considering the situation for a moment the handler, rather than cross the ground which contained the birds, climbed out through a hedge, walked along until level with his dog and climbed into the field again to approach his dog slowly. At the judges' instruction they moved forward and immediately a single partridge rose. After acknowledging the flight the dog continued to road in, firmly taking the air scent of a running bird. After following its tortuous path several yards the bird took flight. Such a classic example of pointing and roading deservedly won the stake, but it was possible only because of the handler's foresight in moving around the unquartered stubble.

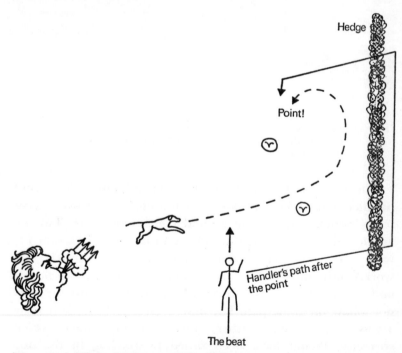

Diag. 18 A difficult situation expertly handled
After the point the handler reached his dog without disturbing the birds. Both birds were raised by the dog on roading forward

8 · WORKING OUT THE POINT

Following a point a dog confirms the presence of birds by roading in to raise them. Thereafter he must ensure no stragglers remain. The purpose of 'working out' the point is to locate and raise any birds which remain in hiding after the main covey has flown.

Working out the point is effected usually by the dog taking short casts about the cover from which the covey rose. When isolated birds are found he points them, moves in, and drops to their flight. Throughout this manœuvre the wise handler keeps his dog under close control with the cautionary command 'to-ho, to-ho', or stays near enough to him to prevent mistakes such as chasing or snapping.

Mistakes are uncommon during the working out of a point. Perhaps the main error is missing a single bird because, when recast, the dog returns hurriedly to the area and flushes the bird in his haste. To avoid such a mishap the handler must ensure that every point, and indeed every flush, is worked out fully before taking up his dog.

Some inexperienced dogs are so fascinated by the scent of birds that they continually return to recent haunts in the hope of detecting yet another bird. Only if the dog is sure no birds have been left behind is the problem easily corrected. Should the handler at a field trial find he is unable to prevent his dog from returning to the area, he is likely to incur a penalty.

At this juncture it may be helpful to the reader to glance at Table 2 which summarizes the five commands, the three whistle signals and the two arm movements required to handle a trained bird dog.

Table 2   A summary of the orders taught to most setters and pointers

	SUGGESTED COMMANDS	USEFUL WHISTLE SIGNALS	POSSIBLE ARM SIGNALS	EXPECTED RESPONSE
I	No	—	—	The dog refrains from committing an error
2	Down or Flat or S-s-s or Hep	A single blast	A raised arm	The dog lies down
3	Name and Come in	Repeated peeps	—	The dog returns to the handler
4	Seek or Get on	—	—	The dog is cast and begins hunting
5	—	Two peeps	Wave the dog across, or point the way	The dog turns through 180° at the end of his lateral cast
6	Move up or Forward	—	—	The dog roads forwards from pointing to raise birds
7	To-ho or Wo, wo, wo, or Steady	—	—	The dog hunts cautiously expecting to find birds nearby, e.g., just prior to the point or when making out a covey

9 · FLUSHING GAME

A dog is said to have flushed birds when he runs so close to them that they are raised and scattered in a disorderly manner. If the flush occurs when the dog is hunting upwind it must be assumed either that he failed to detect the game, in which case the sensitivity of his nose is suspect, or else he flushed the birds deliberately. Both reasons are sufficient to eliminate him from a field trial. When he is running downwind, even if moving cautiously, it is not to be expected that he will scent the game easily. A flush downwind, therefore, does not itself constitute an eliminating fault. Of course, it may develop into one if the dog fails to acknowledge the rising birds by dropping immediately and remaining motionless until the arrival of his handler.

In field trials, before a decision is made about the flushing of birds, a handler or judge must consider the nature of the wind conditions in the area of the mishap. By moving to the spot and there holding a handkerchief to the wind a judge may confirm his opinion of the wind and at the same time demonstrate to the anxious handler the nature of the local conditions. Sometimes, because of the contours of the land, the wind in the region of the flushed birds is blowing in quite a different manner from the wind which the handler or judge, remote from the site, can feel against their face.

A young or inexperienced dog may flush birds at first by drawing slowly into them after detecting their scent a long distance away. This error need cause the handler no alarm for, with practice, the dog will learn the correct distance at which to stand and point his game. In training it is wise to provide him with the opportunity of determining this distance for himself. In field trials, however, a flush can sometimes be prevented by whistling the dog into a down position as soon as he begins to draw forward on a line. An older dog, who is unlikely to flush birds when using an air scent, may run straight into them when he puts his nose down to take their foot scent. Furthermore, so intent does he become in following the line that the handler will find it difficult either to drop him or call him off.

In practice there is rarely any difficulty about deciding if birds have been flushed. The dog is manifestly unprepared for their flight; he makes no attempt to point and, as the birds scatter, he seems both disconcerted and surprised.

In other circumstances, the question of what constitutes a flush may be answered less readily. For example, restless birds, disturbed by some predator or seeking new feeding grounds, may take-off, quite naturally, many yards in front of a working dog. Because the true reasons for their departure cannot be appreciated by the handlers or judges it is possible to assume the dog has precipitated their flight. Such misinterpretation is most likely to be avoided if the judge relates the direction and force of the wind plus the shape of the landscape to the unusual distance at which the covey arose before the dog. By considering whether, under such conditions, birds could reasonably have been detected at that distance the situation is unlikely to be misjudged. However, the decision can be difficult, and calls for much experience if mistakes are to be avoided.

10 · BACKING

A dog is said to 'back' when he voluntarily adopts a pointing attitude at the sight of his brace-mate on point (Plates 5 & 6). Backing serves no useful purpose in locating or raising birds, but it is both a dramatic sight and a valuable discipline, for it enables a handler to concentrate predominantly upon a pointing dog, while his companion remains self-controlled, motionless, and visible. Setters, because they tend naturally to crouch to their game, can sometimes be difficult to see and a following dog may find it harder to back them than animals which stand to their point.

Independence in hunting is an essential quality for a dog to have developed before he is introduced to lessons in backing. If taught at an earlier stage he may never become self-sufficient, always relying on a companion to take the initiative in locating birds. In field trials a discerning judge will soon distinguish a dog who backs but seeks no game actively, from one who backs yet also hunts for himself.

An exercise in basic training which was suggested by one field trialler as a useful preliminary to lessons in backing, involves putting two or even three dogs in a 'down' position, calling them forward individually and dropping them again until they learn to remain steady while a companion passes by or runs ahead (Diagram 19).

Many dogs when introduced to hunting with a brace-mate will turn out to be natural backers. Some, however, have to be taught the art. Lessons necessitate the assistance of an experienced dog who will readily maintain his point. An extra handler can also be most helpful. While the pointing dog is controlled by the helper, the trainer stands behind him restraining his

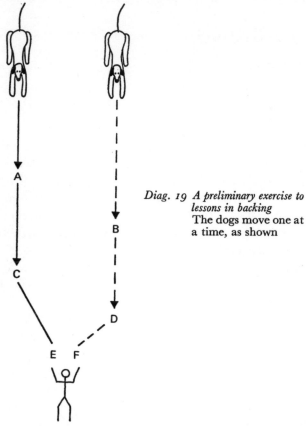

Diag. 19 *A preliminary exercise to
lessons in backing*
The dogs move one at
a time, as shown

inexperienced dog on a check-cord, encouraging his pupil to
stand and watch by gently stroking its back and tail, commanding him quietly to 'stay', and checking any forward movement
with the lead. When working single-handed the trainer must
wait for his older dog to point, then, bringing up his pupil on a
check-line as before, drop him in the backing position. Initially,
the younger dog may attempt to crawl forward as the trainer
advances to control the pointing dog. This creeping movement
must be prevented by using the 'down' command firmly. With
practice, the fixed interest of the first dog will attract the attention of the second until eventually he will rise automatically
from the 'down' position but remain motionless in a pointing

attitude as the advanced dog roads forward. Only when the
pupil is steady to all movement of the dog on point should the
check-line be removed. Thereafter, in time, backing will occur
without any preceding drop, and at increasing distances from
the pointing dog.

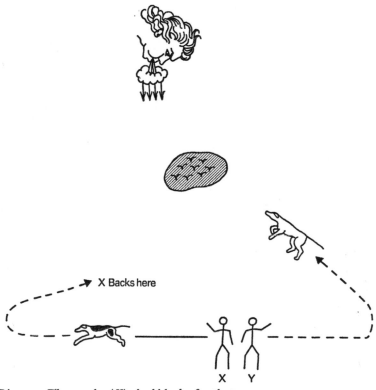

Diag. 20 The rear dog (X) should back after the turn
It will then see the pointing dog

It has been stressed that backing should occur on sight. It
follows that unless the first dog can be seen, the second dog
cannot back him. Thus, in field trials, one member of a brace
who is running away from a dog who comes on point is usually
allowed to complete his cast and given the opportunity of
adopting a backing position before the pointing dog is moved
in (Diagram 20). Similarly, a handler must not expect a dog

taking the forward cast, when his head is turned towards the
wind, to see and back a dog on point behind him (Diagram 21).
Indeed, to prevent the forward dog accidentally spoiling his
companion's find, the handler will have to whistle him down.

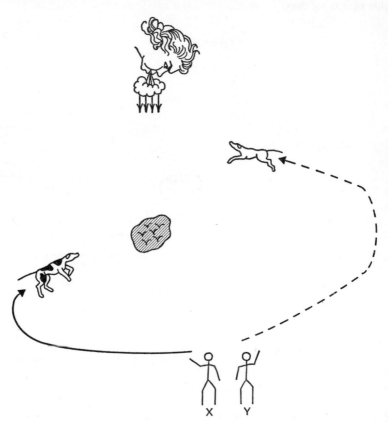

Diag. 21 Backing from the forward dog (Y) cannot be expected
It is not looking at the dog on point

Only when the rear dog can clearly see his brace-mate on
point before him should a natural back be anticipated. However, any necessity to whistle the following dog down in these
circumstances may result in a penalty during field trials. As one
Scottish judge put it, 'One toot, an' yer oot!' Thus, before
whistling a following dog to drop, a handler should ensure that

no slight undulation in the landscape hides the pointing dog from his companion's sight. It is easy to overlook this possibility when, from the handler's higher viewpoint the pointing dog is easily seen.

'Mirror image' backing is an unusual situation which sometimes occurs when, by chance, two dogs approach one another and one pauses to test a whiff of scent. The other promptly backs, whereupon the first dog, having satisfied himself no game is near, looks across to see his companion backing and remains in a backing position himself, assuming, mistakenly, the opposite dog is on point. Watching each other intently both dogs stand locked in this 'mirror image' situation until their handlers lead them away.

11 · JUDGING

The aim of this chapter is to indicate to prospective competitors some of the more widely accepted principles on which field trial judges make their decisions, and the general standard of work to which field triallers try to conform. No attempt has been made to discuss the correctness or incorrectness of any accepted judgements.

In a *Guide to Field Trial Judges issued by the Kennel Club Field Trials Committee*[1] the members of the committee summarize their advice as follows:

> '*Eliminating Faults*: Flushing upwind—Out of control—Chasing fur or feather.
>
> '*Major Faults*: Not quartering and not making ground good—Not dropping to shot—Stickiness on point—Not dropping to flush downwind—Missing birds.
>
> '*Credit Points*: Game finding—Natural backing—Style on point—Pace—Quartering.'

In addition, it is stated elsewhere that, 'noisy handling should be penalized'.

Equally clearly the committee outline a judge's responsibility in the following way, 'The task of judges is to find the dog which, on the day, pleases them most by the quality of its work from the shooting point of view.' One Irish judge expressed a similar thought when he remarked, 'Field trial judges continually ask themselves, "Would the bird be in the bag, and in commonsense did the dog keep to his beat?" '

In field trials for bird dogs there are always two judges to assess the competitions.

[1] *Kennel Club Year Book* (Kennel Club, 1971), p. 221.

Although the purpose of setters and pointers is to locate birds and, without leaving any behind, to raise them in such a way that they may be shot, it is not simply finding birds but how they are found which really matters in competitions. Thus, performance is judged under three headings: ground treatment; game finding ability; handling of birds; all of which are important. Some judges, especially those from Ireland, record their marks on a detailed mark-sheet, like the one shown in Table 3, which includes both credit features and faults.

Meticulous ground treatment—that is, wide, equal and systematic quartering—undertaken with pace and style on either side of a given beat, always creates a favourable impression in field trials. As one judge said, 'Who wants a pointer that footles from side to side? A spaniel makes short casts better and retrieves as well.' Sometimes a judge will indicate the lateral margins of the beat as well as the centre line, inferring thereby that all the ground should be covered. Nevertheless, if handlers interfere too much with their dog's natural casts, solely to comply with such a general directive, they may regret it subsequently. Continual insistence on early turning or longer casts when a dog is hunting can disturb his rhythm and concentration, and result in a disqualifying flush.

Judges are unlikely to select a winning dog who has not amply demonstrated his ability to quarter the ground. Indeed, if game is so plentiful that ground treatment cannot be displayed adequately because of repeated points, successful handlers may be requested at some stage in the competition to hunt their dog across a beat from which all birds have been raised.

Experienced judges quickly recognize errors in pointing, such as false pointing, stealing the point or blinking the point. Also, they are likely to give credit for a normal point only if it is made during the time of judging. Thus, a point obtained unexpectedly—for example, when preparing to cast a dog, or after handlers have been instructed to put their dogs on the lead—rarely obtains marks. On one occasion, after an uninspired run, a dog was ordered in by the judge but his handler attempted to claim a belated and indefinite point. This was

F

Table 3　An example of a judge's mark-sheet for field trials

Stake ....
Breed................ No.........
Handler ....

Quartering		.... Overlooking game
Ground treatment		.... Flushing
Speed		.... Loss of control
Range		.... Chasing
Style of movement		.... Gun shyness
Game finding		.... Handler
Steady to point		.... Back casting
Steady to wing		.... Failure to back
Steady to shot		.... False points
Style of point		.... Pottering
Work out		.... Sticking
Backing		.... Blinking
Obedience		.... Boring

Grade:
Remarks:

ignored. Watching from the crowd, a competitor remarked quietly to his companion, 'It's all in the book now.' His friend agreed, and added a quote from *The Rubaiyat* of Omar Khayyam:

> *The Moving Finger writes; and, having writ,*
> *Moves on; nor all thy Piety nor Wit*
> *Shall lure it back to cancel half a line,*
> *Nor all thy Tears wash out a Word of it.*

'To be sure,' said a passing Irish voice, 'the Bard himself must have been a field trialler!'

To gain marks when roading in, the movement must be performed freely and without hesitation. Extra credit may be obtained if a dog is able to raise his birds in twos or threes at short intervals, thereby providing the guns with time to reload between flights. Such controlled work necessitates the dog being very steady both to shot and to rising game.

When the point appears to be non-productive, roading forward may reasonably continue until the judge decides the dog should be taken up. If, then, the handler is asked whether he wishes to stop or continue, he must look to his dog for some indication of the presence of game nearby. It is unlikely that a dog will be penalized if taken up while still on point, but should the handler permit his dog to move so far forward that the beat is disrupted yet no game is found, he is likely to create an unfavourable impression. Similarly, if, after a long draw forward a dog begins to cast spontaneously, or appears to be following a foot scent only, it is usually wise for the handler to call him in so that he may be formally recast with his brace-mate.

It can happen, when the wind is strong, that a dog with a sensitive nose detects birds so far away that after roading forty yards the point is still unproductive. If, to preserve ground, both dogs are then ordered to be recast and the second dog immediately points birds a short way ahead, it is likely the judge will credit the first dog with the mark 'A+' because his nose was more sensitive, and the second with 'A' because his find was adequate.

Missed birds are a positive sign that a bird dog has made a mistake. Often, however, it does not become obvious that birds have been overlooked until they are raised by the spectators following the competition. Judges usually ignore any birds they happen to notice rising *behind* them assuming, correctly, that other 'missed birds' sometimes fly off which they do not see. By contrast, birds rising *ahead* of the judges but behind dogs which have already quartered the ground are invariably designated 'missed birds', and a fault is always recorded. Sometimes, one of a brace of dogs locates birds after the other has already quartered the ground, thereby providing incontravertible evidence of the first dog's error. Such a fault is not uncommon if, perhaps from jealousy, one animal always takes a wide sweep at the turn to retain a forward cast.

On some occasions a dog who roads forward incautiously permits a running bird to double back and fly up from behind him. Such a bird might be shot in practice but, in field trials, over-running it in such a way constitutes a fault.

After working out the ground recently vacated by a covey of birds, none should be left behind. Dogs which continually return to the site thereafter, rather than proceed with quartering the beat, are usually considered out of control and penalized accordingly.

Judges cannot control the weather. Because of changes in the weather it is inevitable that dogs running late in the competition sometimes have better or worse scenting conditions than earlier competitors. It can also happen that such deterioration occurs in the weather the competition is cancelled, or perhaps judged on one round only. Undoubtedly, in worsening conditions judges prefer to complete a competition whenever possible rather than abandon it. Lunch, therefore, may be curtailed, minor errors may result in the speedy elimination of competitors, and the second round may contain only those dogs with a strong chance of being placed. Even when conditions remain stable throughout the day, judges can make their decisions only on the facts that are available. For example, as it is required that a winning dog must have been shot over, it follows that no matter how excellent his quartering, no matter how obedient he may be, if no birds are available for him to point he cannot easily prove himself steady to the gun and rising game. Despite the wisdom and understanding of judges field triallers need a little help from Lady Luck.

12 · FIELD TRIALS

A field trial is a meeting at which competitions are held for working bird dogs. The winners are usually presented with a trophy and prize money. Prospective trainers interested in obtaining puppies from working stock would be well advised to attend some field trials first, observing dogs for themselves making note of the awards, studying the programmes and discussing possibilities with interested competitors.

Field trial meetings are held in late April and late September, but the major events occur during three weeks of summer prior to August 12th. Most of the clubs under whose auspices the meetings are held are shown in Table 4. The names and addresses of the respective secretaries can be obtained from a copy of the *Kennel Club Year Book* for the current year. Membership of each club is approximately one pound.

Several 'Stakes' (competitions) are held at each field trial. Early in the year the dogs hunt for partridge; for grouse in summer and for pheasant in the autumn. Usually, stakes are confined to one group of dogs, such as 'puppies', which are dogs whelped not earlier than January 1st of the preceding year; 'novices', or sometimes 'non-winners' which, in general, include dogs who have not previously been placed; and 'open' or 'all aged' stakes which are usually for more experienced dogs. Sometimes a 'brace' stake is held, in which instance both dogs must be of the same breed and owned by the same person. Also, once a year a Champion Stake is held in the North or South alternately. A dog which wins a Champion Stake, or alternately two first prizes in the appropriate Open or All Aged Stakes at two different field trials, is entitled to be called a Field Trial Champion.

*Table 4   Some of the clubs promoting field trials for
setters and pointers*

PROMOTING CLUBS	THE SEASON FOR THE MEETING		
English Setter Club	Spring	Summer	—
Kennel Club	Spring	—	—
Southern and Western Counties Field Trial Society	Spring	—	—
Yorkshire Gundog Club	Spring	Summer	—
International Gundog League	—	Summer	Autumn
Pointer Club	—	Summer	—
Irish Setter Association (England) and			
Setter and Pointer Club	—	Summer	—
Scottish Gundog Association	—	Summer	—
Scottish Fields Trial Association	—	Summer	—
Northern Ireland Pointer Club	—	Summer	—
Ulster Irish Red Setter Club	—	Summer	—
Ulster Gundog League	—	Summer	—
Northern Counties Pointer and Setter Society	—	Summer	—
North of Scotland Gundog Association	—	Summer	—

The precise definitions of the various stakes and any restricting clauses are published by the promoting club on a schedule, which is circulated to all interested participants, notifying them of the time and place of a proposed meeting, the order in which stakes will be run, the names of the judges and the closing date for receiving entries and fees. Entry fees vary slightly but, for club members, they are about £2.00 per dog in each stake.

When all the entries have been received and acknowledged by the secretary, dogs are assigned numbers which, prior to the competition, are drawn randomly to determine which dogs shall hunt as a brace and the order of their running. The competition is not of the 'knock-out' type and it is important for newcomers to appreciate that competitors run *with*, not *against* one another. The natural hazards of the competition are more than enough to eliminate the majority of dogs.

To demonstrate pointers or setters to advantage requires a brace of experienced animals and handlers who are quiet and controlled. A dog running wild, or a handler shouting or whistling noisily, disturb and confuse the hunt to such an extent that they eliminate not only themselves but probably their companion also, who cannot concentrate in such mayhem. By contrast, two dogs quartering without jealousy, hunting independently, acknowledging each other's points yet responding promptly to quiet and efficient handlers, cover themselves with glory and pass with high marks into the next round.

During the first round of the competition each brace in turn hunts for about fifteen minutes, their handlers keeping within a reasonable distance of one another as though shooting together. (Sometimes puppies are run for shorter intervals.) If both dogs are of similar appearance they are fitted with distinguishing collars, red for the dog assigned the smaller number, who is usually on the left, and white for the other.

The mid-line of the beat is usually shown to competitors before they cast their dogs, and although gamekeepers do their best to provide each brace with good ground, the precise nature of the terrain and the amount of game it holds is determined mostly by chance.

After dogs have been eliminated from the first round, the numbers of the remaining dogs are drawn randomly in pairs for a second round. Sometimes a third round is also required for which, usually, no draw is necessary as there are so few dogs to be judged.

Suitable clothing for field trials is always advisable. Comfortable walking shoes or light-weight boots, especially if waterproof, are a real asset. Normally jackets, trousers or skirts need to be warm, and dark enough to avoid frightening birds from a distance. Waterproofs are a more difficult problem. It is doubtful if any suitable protective clothing really keeps out heavy rain in the exposed conditions of fields or hillsides. Also, genuine waterproofs are often cumbersome to carry, heavy to wear and sweat so much on the inside that the wearer gets as wet as if the rain had come right through. Most field triallers, therefore, seem to prefer light nylon or plastic waterproofs which can be folded into a pocket and used to keep out winds or showers effectively. Heavier rain soaks everybody, no matter what they wear.

Crooks or walking sticks, used occasionally to chide excitable dogs and referred to by some as 'timely reminders', are found by many competitors to be of assistance. After hours of hard walking they provide a useful leaning post.

Dog leads are kindest to the hands when made of leather, or perhaps a fairly thick pliable rope. Chains or nylon cords chafe the hands by the end of the day. Also, there are fewer willing hands to hold on to a competitor's dogs if leads are unkind to the skin.

Neither leads nor sticks may be carried by a handler whose dog is running before the judges.

Etiquette of the competition

It is understandable if inexperienced competitors feel nervous when taking part in their first field trial. Let them be reassured that many handlers, now renowned, were equally apprehensive at first, and in all probability still feel some nervousness when they are competing. 'Don't you bother,' said one of the old-timers to a newcomer, 'don't you bother yourself. I long since learned just to fill in the forms, drive the bloody car and leave the rest to the dog.'

A few accepted customs are described here which may help the inexperienced competitor to conduct himself with aplomb!

When called before the judges it is helpful to them if the

competitor announces the number assigned to his dog, its sex and breed. These facts may then be checked against the mark-sheet. Next, the two handlers await the judges' instructions regarding the line of the beat and, subsequently, their per-mission to release the dogs. Just prior to casting, the competi-tors usually check with each other that they are both ready to start.

In the excitement of the hunt it is easy for a handler to over-look the fact he is interrupting the quartering of his com-panion's dog by advancing too rapidly (Diagram 22). This oversight should be avoided.

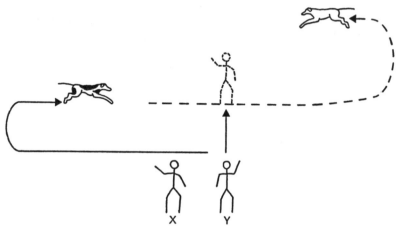

Diag. 22 By moving forward to encourage his dog after it has passed him, handler Y interrupts the path of dog X

Such is the intoxication from the scent of game that when hunting many dogs become excitable as 'the wine goes to their heads'. Yet another feature of their excitement is the sudden necessity to evacuate their bowel! Such an event cannot totally be ignored by either handler, and the accepted compromise is to allow the running dog to complete a forward turn at the end of his cast and, as he approaches the middle of the beat, to whistle him down until the occupied dog can continue.

Should a dog come on point it is sporting for his handler to mention the fact quietly to the other competitor, who may have missed the fact. This enables the second dog to be handled into a backing position. It also avoids him flushing birds accidentally on his next cast across.

In all circumstances at field trials, handlers should be as decisive as possible. If uncertainty surrounds one competitor, the other may whistle down his dog to determine the problem. A fruitless situation is then recognized and the hunt continues. After two or three such instances, the dogs become restless and disobedient. Indeed, a handler who twice whistles his dog down for no good reason may subsequently choose to ignore any further indecision on the part of his companion, even at the risk of a stolen point or a flush.

When a point is claimed, especially if backed closely by another dog, the handler of the first dog normally takes care

Diag. 23 To approach his dog (X) handler X moves cautiously behind the backing dog (Y), not alongside it

how he approaches his animal. He joins him quietly and cautiously, ensuring he does not inadvertently disturb or interrupt the concentration of his companion's dog by moving in front of him (Diagram 23). Without such caution the backing dog may start to road forward as the first handler walks past him. Having arrived by his dog, the front handler does not usually begin roading forward until the handler of the backing dog has had time to get near enough to his animal to control it.

The unwritten courtesies of field trials do much to keep the standard of the competitions high. They are based solely on a consideration for the other man. In practice they make hunting with bird dogs one of the most noble, the most exciting and the most gentlemanly of all field sports.